DATE D

U.S. SPECIAL OPS

STORIES
FROM THOSE WHO FOUGHT IN
AMERICA'S
SPECIAL OPS

by Amie Jane Leavitt

Consultant:
Raymond L. Puffer, PhD
Historian, Retired
Edwards Air Force Base History Office

CAPSTONE PRESS
a capstone imprint

Connect is published by
Capstone Press,
1710 Roe Crest Drive, North Mankato, Minnesota 56003
www.mycapstone.com

Library of Congress Cataloging-in-Publication Data
Names: Leavitt, Amie Jane, author.
Title: Stories from those who fought in America's Special Ops / by Amie Jane
   Leavitt.
Description: North Mankato, Minnesota : Capstone Press, 2017. | Series:
   Connect. U.S. Special Ops | Includes bibliographical references and index.
   | Audience: Ages 8–14. | Audience: Grade 4 to 6.
Identifiers: LCCN 2016010280 | ISBN 9781515718512 (library binding) | ISBN
   9781515718543 (eBook PDF)
Subjects: LCSH: Special operations (Military science)—United
   States—Juvenile literature. | Special forces (Military science)—United
   States—Juvenile literature.
Classification: LCC UA34.S64 L43 2017 | DDC 356/.16092273—dc23
LC record available at https://lccn.loc.gov/2016010280

Editorial Credits
Brenda Haugen, editor; Steve Mead, designer; Jo Miller, media researcher;
Katy LaVigne, production specialist

Image Credits
Alamy: North Wind Picture Archives, 8, Roberto Nistri, 37; Bridgeman
Images: Museum of the Confederacy, Richmond, Virginia, USA/Photo ©
Civil War Archive, 14–15, Private Collection/© Look and Learn, 10–11; Getty
Images: AFP/Dan De Luce, 40, AFP/Johnny Eggit, 36, Archive Photos/MPI/
Wall, cover, Bettmann, 27, 31, 32–33, Hulton Archive/Galeria Bilderwelt,
24–25, The LIFE Picture Collection/Cari Mydans, 28, The LIFE Picture
Collection/Time Life Pictures/US Navy, 39, UIG/Photo12, 23, Underwood
Archives, 16–17, 18–19; Glow Images: Superstock, 6–7; Newscom: Everett
Collection, 21, imageBROKER/Michael Szönyl, 4; Shutterstock: Everett
Historical, 13, 15 (inset), Paladin12, 9; U.S Air Force photo by Staff Sgt.
Douglas Ellis, 44; Wikimedia: Bundeswehr/Mandt, 34–35, Official U.S. Navy
photo by PH2 Eric S. Logsdon, Naval Special Warfare Command Public
Affairs Office, 42, Pete Souza, Official White House Photographer, 43

Design Elements
Shutterstock: mcherevan, Nik Merkulov, Yulia Glam

Printed and bound in Canada.
009649F16

TABLE OF CONTENTS

★☆☆☆

CHAPTER 1

THE BEST OF THE BEST

After the Americans captured Fort Ticonderoga in northern New York during the Revolutionary War (1775–1783), General George Washington asked Henry Knox and his men to complete a special mission. They were to retrieve 59 British cannons and **mortars** from the fort and transport them across water and land to Boston, Massachusetts. The distance was about 300 miles (483 kilometers). The mission was important. The cannons were needed to defend Boston. It was one of the first Continental Army Special Operations missions undertaken by the young nation.

 Today Fort Ticonderoga is a museum and is recognized as a National Historic Landmark.

Knox wrote to Washington and described the amount of effort it took to complete the mission: "It is not easy to conceive the difficulties we have had in getting them over the Lake owing to the advanced Season of the Year & contrary winds—three days ago it was very uncertain whether we could have gotten them over untill next Spring, but now please God they shall go—I have had made forty two exceeding strong sleds & have provided eighty yoke of Oxen to drag them as far as Springfield."

Through the years members of U.S. military Special Operations units have been **elite**. Their members are strong, fast, intelligent, and able to survive in extreme conditions. They perform some of the toughest and most important jobs. Special Operations units help maintain national security by getting important information from behind enemy lines. Quite often, they put themselves in harm's way by rescuing military members and civilians who have been captured by enemies. They also fight enemies wherever they are called to around the world.

Get up close and personal with Special Operations personnel and those familiar with their work. Learn about everything from training and tools to first-hand accounts of some of their biggest missions.

mortar—a short cannon that fires bombs or projectiles high in the air

elite—a group of people who have special advantages or talents

★ ★ ★ ☆ ☆

CHAPTER 2

THE EARLY DAYS OF U.S. SPECIAL OPS

One of the first Special Operations units that fought on the American continent battled on the side of the British during the French and Indian War (1754–1763). They were called Rogers' Rangers, which was named for the man who organized them, Robert Rogers.

Rogers' Rangers were basically backwoodsmen. They were men who lived in the wild **frontier** as hunters and trappers. They knew how to shoot remarkably well. In order to stay alive in such a wild, untamed environment as the American frontier, they had to be excellent marksmen.

When Rogers formed the group, he was ordered by his superior to only enlist men who were "used to travelling and hunting, and in whose courage and fidelity I could confide."

 Jean Leon Gerome Ferris depicted Rogers' Rangers in this 1758 painting.

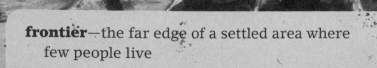

frontier—the far edge of a settled area where few people live

EARLY MISSIONS

Robert Rogers kept a journal. In the journal, Rogers wrote about various missions during the French and Indian War. He included details about one mission in which the Rangers captured a sawmill:

« an illustration of Robert Rogers

I marched, agreeable to orders from the General, across the mountains in the isthmus; from thence, in a byway, athwart the woods to the bridge at the sawmills; where finding the bridge standing, I immediately crossed it with my Rangers, and took possession of the rising ground on the other side, and beat from thence a party of the enemy, and took several prisoners, killed others, and put the remainder to flight, before Col. Haviland with his grenadiers and light infantry got over. The army took possession that night of the heights near the sawmills, where they lay all this evening.

SECRECY AT SEA

Rogers' Rangers inspired people to form similar groups during the Revolutionary War (1775–1783), including the famous Knowlton Rangers organized by George Washington. On one occasion, Washington wrote about one corps of riflemen led by Commander Daniel Morgan from the colony of Virginia: "These are all chosen Men, selected from the Army at large—well acquainted with the use of Rifles and with that mode of Fighting which is necessary to make them a good Counterpoise [balance] to the Indians.... I expect the most eminent services from them."

Many Special Operations missions have taken place on the water. Rogers' Rangers, for example, were excellent marksmen and knew their way around the woods. However, in New England, where they mainly fought, they spent a lot of time on water, **covertly** moving across lakes and rivers. In a pinch, Rogers' Rangers knew how to build their own rafts and used blankets for sails. They also used birch bark canoes, the main water transportation used by American Indians, and cedar whaleboats.

Rogers' Rangers used the forest to their advantage when ambushing their enemies.

LEARNING FROM THE AMERICAN INDIANS

Today's U.S. Special Operations units that battle on land owe many of their survival techniques to the early American Indians. The American Indians were truly the first **guerrilla** fighters. They knew the importance of wearing clothing that blended in with their environment. They didn't foolishly march out into the open and make themselves targets. Instead, they wisely hid behind trees and rocks and sneaked up on their enemy. Their techniques helped the American Indians survive in their wild environment. These same **tactics** continue to help Special Ops units as they battle their enemies in all kinds of **terrain**.

covert—secret

guerrilla—a member of a small group of fighters or soldiers

tactic—a plan for fighting a battle

terrain—the surface of the land

CIVIL WAR SPECIAL OPS

Though John Mosby spoke against secession, he joined the **Confederate** army after the Civil War (1861–1865) began. He became part of a group called the Virginia Volunteers, a company of infantry that fought on horseback.

Mosby quickly showed amazing skill in gathering **intelligence**. In January 1863 Mosby was put in charge of the 43rd Virginia Calvary, which came to be known as Mosby's Rangers. They conducted lightning fast raids on **Union** supply lines and harassed those carrying messages for the Union. Mosby's Rangers grew more famous with each success, as did their leader. Mosby became known as "The Gray Ghost" because of his ability to seemingly appear and disappear as he pleased.

"It is a classical maxim that it is sweet and becoming to die for one's country; but whoever has seen the horrors of a battlefield feels that it is far sweeter to live for it."

—former Confederate Colonel John Mosby

Confederate—the southern states that fought against the northern states in the Civil War

intelligence—secret information about an enemy's plans or actions

Union—the northern states that fought against the southern states in the Civil War

Colonel John Mosby

In March 1863 Mosby's Rangers conducted their most famous and most daring raid. Mosby and 30 of his troops rode inside Union lines at Fairfax County Court House, Virginia, and captured Union General Edwin Stoughton as he slept. Finding the general in bed, Mosby slapped him on the rear and asked, "Do you know Mosby, General?" The general responded, "Yes! Have you got the rascal?" "No," Mosby replied. "He's got you!"

soldiers in Mosby's Rangers

Mosby was so important to the Confederacy that many Union officers tried to capture him. They all failed. Robert E. Lee, as commander of the army of northern Virginia, knew how valuable Mosby was. "I wish I had 100 men like Mosby," Lee is said to have remarked.

Robert E. Lee

★★★☆

CHAPTER 3

WORLD WAR II

"We'd go in, we had explosives, TNT... it's a slow explosive. It's not like dynamite. Dynamite goes off very fast.... We'd swim in with this explosive on our backs. And if we found anything in there that had to be blown out, we'd attach [the explosives] to it, got away as fast as we could, and set it, and it would go off.... At Iwo Jima, we cleared [the beach] one day, and then the Marines got there the next day."

— Ramon Vanderwalker, World War II frogman, on clearing obstacles

FROGMEN OF WWII

Before the Navy SEALs were born, the Navy Combat Demolition Units, nicknamed frogmen, did similar work during World War II (1939–1945). Frogmen were trained in swimming and **scuba** diving, mainly in the ocean. They also received underwater demolition training (UDT). Frogmen would go in first to a beach landing area and blow up obstacles that could be dangerous to landing craft. These obstacles could be natural, such as coral reefs and shoals, or defensives, such as mines and cables, placed there by the enemy. Frogmen often swam in the dark of night. These early demolition crews didn't have the elaborate uniforms and equipment today's Navy SEALs do. Frogmen often swam in only a pair of swim trunks and carried explosives and knives as their only gear.

scuba—self-contained underwater breathing apparatus, based on a device that uses a tank of compressed gas (usually air) for diving

Coxswain Calvin Byrd, a World War II frogman, talked about the training they underwent.

"Lessons were given in the use of rubber boats for landing from PT boats and submarines. We practiced landing on beaches in the surf, pulling boats ashore, deflating them so they could be hidden in the jungle, and later inflating them with a small cylinder of compressed air for the return after the mission was completed.

Navy UDT teams continued after WWII.

...We made many trips into the jungle for stays of two or three days or more. We landed at night along the coast. We had classes on what intelligence was likely to be gathered.

...We played physical fitness exercises such as five-mile fast marches. We learned to communicate with the natives. We had target practice with our carbines and .45 pistols."

D-DAY

For 20 months the Army Rangers in the 116th Infantry prepared for one of their most crucial missions of World War II. During intense drills the Rangers practiced landing on beaches through difficult waters. They practiced climbing rope ladders up steep, rocky cliffs. They worked hard to develop speed and accuracy in all of their maneuvers.

The day for action had finally arrived—June 6, 1944. It was D-Day. When the Allied soldiers made their massive invasion on the French coast in the early morning hours, the Rangers' mission was to strike one particularly important post. It was called Pointe du Hoc, and it was the place where the Germans had stationed a defensive post of heavy **artillery** pieces. If the guns were not taken over, the Germans could stop the Allied invasion. The Rangers had to be successful. The entire D-Day invasion of Normandy depended upon it.

Before landing on the beach, Rangers were packed shoulder to shoulder on a small landing craft.

artillery—cannons and other large guns
designed to strike an enemy from a distance

The Rangers' mission was to land on the beach, shoot grappling hooks with rope ladders to the top of the cliffs, then climb 100 feet (30.5 m) up the sheer cliff. Once they reached the top of the cliff, they were to take out the Germans and their guns on top of Pointe du Hoc.

"I got in the boat, and when we pulled away the water was rough, and it was cold and as we came in closer and closer to the shore, that's when we start seeing these [rockets] flying over the top of us.... By that time, I had thrown up through my vomit bag.... My job was to hook the grappling hook on the rockets to fire the rope up the cliff.... The last thing I said to myself ... [or rather] to the guy upstairs was, 'Dear God, don't let me drown. I want to get in and do what I'm supposed to do.'"

—Sergeant Antonio T. Ruggiero, D Company, 2nd Ranger **Battalion**

battalion—unit of soldiers in the armed forces or emergency forces

Pointe du Hoc on D-Day

Sergeant Leonard G. Lomell, D Company, 2nd Ranger Battalion, remembered:

"We landed and fired off our rockets, the ramp goes down, and I'm the first guy shot in the company, a machine gun through the right side. Then I stepped off into water over my head, and the guys pulled me out, and we just rushed to the base of that cliff and grabbed any rope we could get, and up the cliff we went just as fast as we could go. The wound wasn't bad. It had gone through the muscle on my right side.... [Finally at the top,] as we rushed them, we got to the gun positions where we were assigned, but there were no guns.... They gotta be here. We went down this one sunken road, and we saw what looked to be wagon wheel tracks.... I looked over and there was an apple orchard. And there, lo and behold, were the guns of Pointe du Hoc."

after the assault at Pointe du Hoc by the 2nd Ranger Battalion

HIGGINS BOATS

Many of the American troops arrived at the beaches of Normandy in LCVPs (Landing Craft Vehicle Personnel). Nicknamed Higgins Boats after their inventor, businessman Andrew Higgins, the LCVPs held up to 36 men plus a crew. They were outfitted with three pairs of rockets. One pair of rockets fired grapnels that could hold ropes or ladders to the top of the cliffs.

THE GREAT RAID

On January 30, 1945, Special Operations troops and local soldiers planned a daring nighttime operation of World War II. Their target was the Cabanatuan prisoner of war (POW) camp in the Philippines. The U.S. Army 6th Ranger Battalion, the Alamo Scouts, and Filipino guerrillas worked together to rescue 513 Allied POWs during the World War II raid. Many of these soldiers were survivors from the infamous Bataan Death March. "The Great Raid," as this mission is now called, is considered one of the most successful rescue missions in U.S. history.

The U.S. Rangers arrived on the island of Luzon in the Philippines in late January 1945. They began consulting with guerrillas there January 27. The next day the Rangers began crossing 30 miles (48 km) into enemy territory. About 1,000 Japanese soldiers camped near the prison and another 7,000 were stationed nearby. Along the way, the Rangers had to brave a variety of terrain, including crossing a river. They used the dense tropical jungle to remain hidden.

BATAAN DEATH MARCH

On April 9, 1942, the United States surrendered the Bataan Peninsula in the Philippines to the Japanese. About 75,000 American and Filipino troops on Bataan were forced to march 65 miles (105 km) to the Japanese prison camps. The intense heat and brutal treatment by the Japanese guards made the journey even more miserable. Thousands died in what came to be called the Bataan Death March.

"I'd glance up on occasion and could see the ... guards in the watchtowers. I said a prayer, 'Please, God, don't let them see us.'"
—Ranger August T. Stern, Jr.

some of the rescued Americans from Cabanatuan POW camp

Two teams of Alamo Scouts gathered intelligence about the Japanese movements on the island. Two scouts, dressed like locals in straw hats and farm clothes, sneaked into a hut overlooking the camp. From this vantage point, they were able to figure out the best route for the Rangers to take into the camp to rescue the POWs.

The Rangers began their raid at nightfall on January 30, 1945. Since the land around the camp was so flat, they knew they couldn't get to the camp without being seen. The U.S. Army Air Force arranged for a P-61 Black Widow to fly over the camp at just the right moment.

"The P-61 was one of the biggest factors maintaining our surprise," said Captain Robert Prince, the Ranger company commander.

While the Japanese guards looked up into the sky, the Rangers began their approach on the camp. They crawled on their bellies through a dry rice paddy until they reached the entrances. Some came in toward the front of the camp and some from the rear. They were joined by Filipino guerrilla groups, villagers, and the Alamo Scouts.

The men burst through the doors in a shower of machine gun fire. The Japanese guards were taken by surprise, and the Rangers were able to take immediate control of the camp. Within 30 minutes, the raid was over. Most of the POWs inside the camp were rescued, though at least one of the prisoners died during the rescue. Many were so ill that they had to be carried out on the Rangers' backs.

"I think I was the first American out of the prison camp," a former prisoner recalled. "First thing I knew was I was standing outside with a big Yank [American]. His name was Captain Prince of Seattle, Washington. The first thing I did was to grab the captain and hug and kiss him right there."

the 6th Ranger Battalion and Filipino guerillas

★★★★

CHAPTER 4

MODERN MISSIONS

OPERATION KINGPIN

"We were not forgotten; our country cared!"
—a prisoner of war talking about how he felt after
Operation Kingpin

By late November 1970, a mission during the
Vietnam War required Special Operations. Operation
Kingpin had the green light. Kingpin was a joint
service operation that involved a Navy aircraft carrier,
56 handpicked Army Special Forces soldiers, and an
Air Force assault group.

After practicing the mission for months at Eglin Air
Force Base in Florida, the Special Forces teams were
ready to roll. Their mission: to rescue as many as 55
POWs held at Son Tay POW Camp, located 23 miles
(37 km) west of the North Vietnamese capital of Hanoi.
The aircraft left Thailand on the evening of November
20 with plans of reaching Son Tay in the early morning
hours. At the same time, planes from the Navy aircraft
carrier created a diversion in the Haiphong area.
The first helicopter destroyed the guard towers and
the **barracks**. The second helicopter landed in the
center of the camp and delivered Army Special Forces
soldiers, which are sometimes called Green Berets. The
third helicopter landed outside the camp and delivered

more Green Berets. Once inside the camp, the Special Forces teams were surprised by something they didn't expect. The camp was empty of prisoners. They had been moved to another location.

⩔ Son Tay POW Camp in North Vietnam

barracks—buildings where soldiers sleep on military bases

Even though they didn't rescue any prisoners, the Son Tay Raid was not a failure. It showed the North Vietnamese that the United States would do what was necessary to rescue their POWs. It also sent a positive message to the POWs—they were not forgotten.

In an interview, Sergeant Terry Buckler, a member of the Special Forces team during the Son Tay Raid, talked about the training before the mission:

President Richard Nixon presented medals of gallantry to the Special Forces team that executed the Son Tay Raid.

"We had a mockup of Son Tay.... We started training in the daytime, going through dry runs. We practiced our positioning and what to do when our choppers hit the ground. There were three ships [helicopters]—one Sikorsky HH-3 Jolly Green Giant and two HH-53 Super Jollies—going in; Greenleaf, Blueboy, and Redwine were their radio call signs. Then we began doing night training. There was a flare ship above us that lit up the compound. We used live ammunition the entire time as well."

BEHIND ENEMY LINES

An F-16 fighter pilot, Captain Scott O'Grady, was shot down by a Serbian missile over the wooded countryside of northern Bosnia on June 2, 1995. The missile cut his jet in two. O'Grady ejected from his seat and parachuted out of the wreckage as it tumbled to the ground.

Though he suffered just minor burns and cuts, O'Grady was in immediate danger when he landed. He was in a warzone, and the Serbians were anxious to get their hands on him.

O'Grady stayed out of sight during the daytime hours and only moved about at night. He had no food, so he ate insects to stay alive.

"My primary goal was to not get caught by the enemy."

—Captain Scott O'Grady

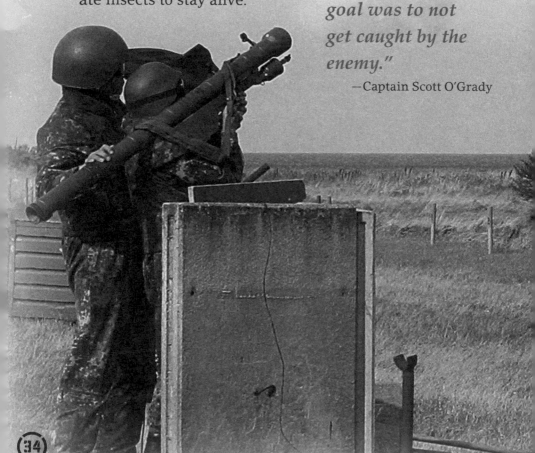

In his survival kit, O'Grady had an emergency beacon with a radio signal that could transmit his exact location. He kept trying to use the beacon, but the signal only travelled about 40 miles (64 km). On his fifth night on the ground, O'Grady climbed a nearby hill hoping the signal could travel farther from that position.

During the time O'Grady was missing, the U.S. military was searching for him. When O'Grady climbed the hill, they finally caught his signal around 2:30 a.m.

"Basher 5-2, this is Basher 1-1. You're loud and clear," said a fellow fighter pilot over the radio to O'Grady using their code names.

When O'Grady heard those words, he just wanted to scream with relief. "I'm alive," he replied in the radio. "I'm alive."

"I'd been dead to the outside world for six days," O'Grady later told a reporter. "Now, I knew the cavalry was on the way."

◀ A missile like the one shown shot down Captain Scott O'Grady's fighter plane.

The map shows where U.S. Marines rescued Captain Scott O'Grady.

Within three hours a TRAP team (Tactical Recovery of Aircraft and Personnel) of 41 Marines was flying toward Bosnia to rescue O'Grady. It was already daylight when they neared his location, which made the rescue more dangerous for everyone.

Fog crept into the countryside that morning, making it more difficult to find O'Grady. But they finally did. Once the TRAP team secured his location, they lowered the two helicopters to the ground, and O'Grady started running toward them.

"Seeing him running through the brush, covered in sweat with a six-day beard on his face and his pistol in his hand is a scene I'll never forget," said the mission commander Lieutenant Colonel Chris Gunther. "I said to myself, 'He looks good and moves pretty good for someone who's been on the ground for six days.'"

36

When O'Grady was safely on board, they hurriedly lifted off the ground. Although the flight into Bosnia had been uneventful, the flight back was anything but. The fog had lifted by that point, which also made the helicopters visible to the enemy. Shots rang out.

"I saw a Russian-made SA-7 fire at us," said the co-pilot Captain Jim Wright. "It came corkscrewing up at us from the left side of the aircraft."

To avoid being hit, they flew in unpredictable ways.

"We were zigzagging around, banking hard all over the place," said Lance Corporal Paul Bruce. "The roughest helicopter ride I've ever been on."

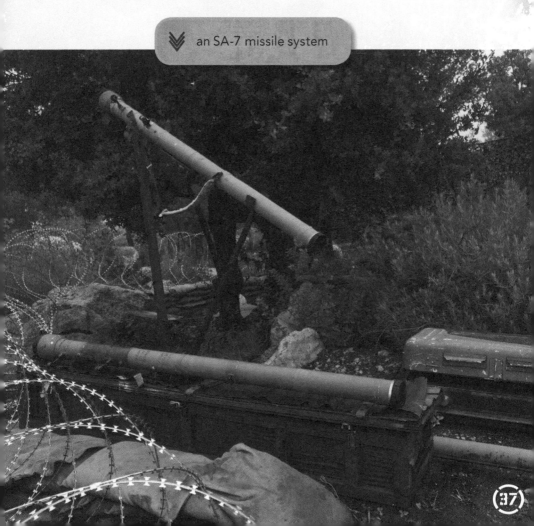

an SA-7 missile system

But they finally made it. Five hours after the rescue mission began, they were all safely onboard the USS *Kearsarge* in the Adriatic Sea.

Secretary of the Navy John H. Dalton responded to O'Grady's rescue:

Fortune favors the bold, and there is no bolder force than the Navy and Marine Corps team. During the past week, all Americans and our allies have been praying for the young Air Force pilot shot down over Bosnia. The Marines of the 24th MEU (SOC) and all sailors and Marines aboard the USS Kearsarge answered those prayers and proved yet again that ours is the finest naval service in the world.... I am extremely proud of all our Navy and Marine Corps forces now deployed in the Adriatic. You are faced with a difficult situation, and you are performing superbly. Remain focused on the task at hand and sail proudly. God bless you.

Captain Scott O'Grady after being rescued from enemy territory

FINDING PUBLIC ENEMY NO. 1

Dawn had yet to arrive May 2, 2011. The night was pitch black, as black as the Black Hawk helicopters nearing Abbottabad, Pakistan. The Pakistani town was home to Osama bin Laden. Bin Laden was America's Public Enemy No. 1—the mastermind behind the 9/11 terror attacks in the United States. The **terrorist** was hiding in a **compound** in the foothills of a mountainous region.

Yet the dark night didn't make any difference to the 23 men from U.S. Navy SEAL Team 6 and the pilots who assisted them during Operation Neptune Spear. The U.S. Army 160th Special Operations Aviation Regiment,

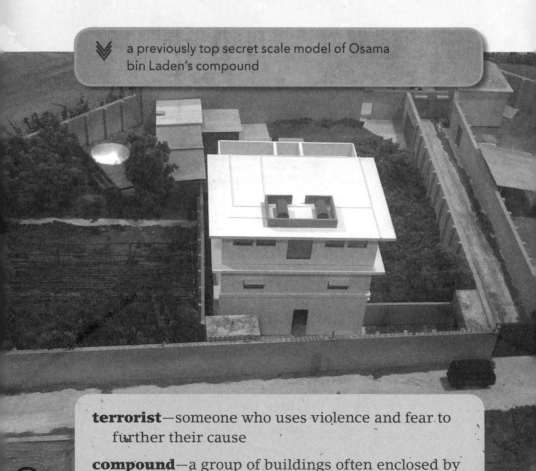

a previously top secret scale model of Osama bin Laden's compound

terrorist—someone who uses violence and fear to further their cause

compound—a group of buildings often enclosed by a fence or a wall

THE RIGHT VEHICLE FOR THE JOB

Black Hawk helicopters are used by the military's Special Operations forces. The helicopters travel at a top speed of 183 miles (295 km) per hour. They are 65 feet (20 meters) long. Their rotor blades give the aircraft a wingspan of 54 feet (16.5 m). A typical Black Hawk helicopter costs around $21.3 million. The top-secret, never-before-seen helicopters used during the bin Laden raid cost even more. They had been specially designed to mask heat, noise, and movement. The aircrafts' exteriors also had sharp, flat angles and were covered with radar-dampening "skin" to avoid detection.

known as Night Stalkers, provided the helicopters and the pilots. The U.S. Navy SEALs provided the manpower.

Two Black Hawk helicopters descended on the complex. One had to make an emergency crash landing. Luckily, no one was injured onboard the crashed Black Hawk. With the helicopter unable to be used for the flight back, the SEALs destroyed the Black Hawk with explosives.

The SEALs hopped out of the helicopter and hurried into the compound. With night vision goggles, the men were easily able to scan the shadowy rooms as they hunted for their target: Osama bin Laden.

"This is it. This is why we're here. We are at war because of this guy and now we are going to go get him."

— Rob O'Neill, Navy SEAL who was on the Osama bin Laden raid

The American sailors were dressed in camouflage and protective gear. They carried either an M4 rifle or a Heckler & Koch MP7.

When bin Laden's guards awoke and scrambled into action, shots rang out in the compound. But bin Laden's guards were too slow to react and were no match for the Navy SEALs. The SEALs killed some of bin Laden's men before climbing the stairs in the building.

By the time the guards with bin Laden were alerted, the SEALs had already located bin Laden in an upstairs bedroom. Seconds after bin Laden was discovered, shots were fired. Bin Laden was dead.

Navy SEALs in full gear

members of the National Security Team watching live video of the Osama bin Laden raid

The SEALs radioed back to their commanders. "For God and country—Geronimo, Geronimo, Geronimo," they said. "Geronimo E.K.I.A." They spoke with their **encrypted** message—"Enemy Killed in Action," their message meant.

SEAL Rob O'Neill claimed to be the man who shot bin Laden. He later talked about what it felt like to be part of such an important mission: "To be part of something so historic, you can't ask for more...."

encrypt—to encode a message in such a way that only certain people can understand it

MAKING A MARK IN THE WORLD

Much of the work of the U.S. military's Special Forces is done in secret. They don't do their jobs for fame or fortune. They do their jobs because they love their country and want to make the world a safer place. Glimpses into their training and missions through the history of the nation show the importance of their work. They've helped not only the United States, but other countries around the globe.

 U.S. Air Force soldier jumping out of an MC-130J Combat Shadow II during a training exercise.

artillery (ar-TIL-uh-ree)—cannons and other large guns designed to strike an enemy from a distance

battalion (buh-TAL-yuhn)—unit of soldiers in the armed forces or emergency forces

barracks (BAR-uhks)—buildings where soldiers sleep on military bases

compound (KAHM-pownd)—a group of buildings often enclosed by a fence or a wall

Confederate (Kuhn-FE-der-uht)—the southern states that fought against the northern states in the Civil War

covert (koh-VURT)—secret

eject (i-JEKT)—to force one's way out

elite (i-LEET)—a group of people who have special advantages or talents

encrypt (en-KRIPT)—to encode a message in such a way that only certain people can understand it

frontier (fruhn-TEER)—the far edge of a settled area where few people live

guerrilla (guh-RIL-ah)—a member of a small group of fighters or soldiers

intelligence (in-TEL-uh-jenss)—secret information about an enemy's plans or actions

interrogation (in-TAYR-uh-gay-shuhn)—the questioning of someone formally and thoroughly

mortar (MOR-tur)—a short cannon that fires bombs or projectiles high in the air

reconnaissance (ree-KAH-nuh-suhnss)—a mission to gather information about an enemy

scuba (SKOO-bah)—self-contained underwater breathing apparatus, based on the device developed by Emile Gagnan and Jacques Cousteau, which uses a tank of compressed gas (usually air) for diving

tactic (TAK-tik)—a plan for fighting a battle

terrain (tuh-RAYN)—the surface of the land

terrorist (TER-ur-ist)—someone who uses violence and fear to further their cause

Union (YOON-yuhn)—the northern states that fought against the southern states in the Civil War

ADDITIONAL RESOURCES

READ MORE

Leavitt, Amie Jane. *U.S. Navy by the Numbers.* Military by the Numbers. North Mankato, Minn.: Capstone Press, 2014.

Nardo, Don. *Special Operations: Reconnaissance.* The Military Experience. Greensboro, N.C.: Morgan Reynolds Pub., 2013.

Sodaro, Craig. *The U.S. Marines Special Operations Regiment: The Missions.* American Special Ops. North Mankato, Minn.: Capstone Press, 2013.

INTERNET SITES

FactHound offers a safe, fun way to find Internet sites related to this book. All of the sites on FactHound have been researched by our staff.

Here's all you do:
Visit *www.facthound.com*
Type in this code: 9781515718512

CRITICAL THINKING USING THE COMMON CORE

1. What did other Special Operations groups learn from the Rangers? (Key Ideas and Details)

2. Do you think you would be a good special operator? Why or why not? What kind of missions would fit you best? (Integration of Knowledge and Ideas)

3. How did the tools used by Confederate and Union soldiers aid them on their missions? What would you change or add to help them do their work better? (Integration of Knowledge and Ideas)

Chapter 1

Page 5, line 3: The Gilder Lehrman Institute of American History. Dragging cannon from Fort Ticonderoga to Boston, 1775. 18 April 2016. http://www.gilderlehrman.org/history-by-era/war-for-independence/resources/dragging-cannon-from-fort-ticonderoga-boston-1775

Chapter 2

Page 7, line 2: Chris McNab, ed. America's Elite: US Special Forces from the American Revolution to the Present Day. New York: Osprey Publishing, 2014, Kindle Edition, p. 210.

Page 9, line 1: Robert Rogers. Journals of Major Robert Rogers: Containing an Account of the Several Excursions He Made Under the Generals Who Commanded Upon the Continent of North America, During the Late War. Albany, New York: Joel Munsell's Sons, 1883, p.136.

Page 12: McNab, p.356.

Page 14, line 6: Civil War Trust. John Singleton Mosby. 25 April 2016. http://www.civilwar.org/education/history/biographies/john-singleton-mosby.html

Page 15, line 7: Kathleen Golden. Smithsonian. "Meet John S. Mosby, 'Gray Ghost' of the Confederacy." Published 6 December 2013. Retrieved 25 April 2016. http://americanhistory.si.edu/blog/2013/12/meet-john-s-mosby-the-gray-ghost-of-the-confederacy.html

Chapter 3

Page 16, line 1: Sealexperience. Navy Seal BUD/S WWII UDT Frogman Interview. Don Shipley interviews a Iwo Jima Veteran UDT Frogman. Published 29 November 2011. Retrieved 25 April 2016. https://www.youtube.com/watch?v=nKVkUjiJS6Y

Page 18, line 3: Chet Cunningham. The Frogman of World War II. An Oral History of the U.S. Navy's Underwater Demolition Units. New York: Simon Schuster, 2005, p. 9.

Page 20, line 1: ABMCVIDEOS. Stories of Pointe du Hoc. 25 April 2016. https://www.youtube.com/watch?v=CyQw6DAP9v8

Page 24, line 3: PBS. American Experience. Voices of D-Day: Leonard Lomell. 25 April 2016. http://www.pbs.org/wgbh/amex/dday/sfeature/sf_voices_06.html

Page 27, line 1: Frederick Rasmussen. "A film recalls a daring – and largely forgotten – rescue mission." Baltimore Sun. Published 24 September 2005. Retrieved 25 April 2016. http://articles.baltimoresun.com/2005-09-24/news/0509240087_1_pows-6th-ranger-great-raid

Page 28, line 14: PBS. Bataan Rescue. People & Events: Robert Prince and the Raid. 25 April 2016. http://www.pbs.org/wgbh/amex/bataan/peopleevents/e_raid.html

Page 29, line 16: Mike Barber. "Leader of WWII's 'Great Raid' looks back at real-life POW rescue." SeattlePi. Published 24 April 2005. Retrieved 25 April 2016. http://www.seattlepi.com/local/article/Leader-of-WWII-s-Great-Raid-looks-back-at-1181340.php

Chapter 4

Page 30, line 1: National Museum of the US Air Force. Rescue Attempt: The Son Toy Raid. 25 April 2016. http://www.nationalmuseum.af.mil/Visit/MuseumExhibits/FactSheets/Display/tabid/509/Article/196019/rescue-attempt-the-son-tay-raid.aspx

Page 33, line 1: History.net. Interview with Sergeant Terry Buckler About the Son Tay Prison Camp Raid During the Vietnam War. 25 April 2016. http://www.historynet.com/interview-with-sergeant-terry-buckler-about-the-son-tay-prison-camp-raid-during-the-vietnam-war.htm

Page 34: Daniel Snyder. Documentary: To the Rescue (excerpt). Published 12 Aug 2010. Retrieved 25 April 2016. https://www.youtube.com/watch?v=2QhulhJsrWM

Page 35, line 12: Ross W. Simpson. "The Rescue of 'Basher 52'." Marine Corps Association & Foundation. Published September 1995. Retrieved 25 April 2016. https://www.mca-marines.org/leatherneck/rescue-basher-52

Page 36, line 11: Fox News. "Man who shot Usama bin Laden speaks out in exclusive Fox News interview." Published 12 November 2014. Retrieved 25 April 2016. http://www.foxnews.com/us/2014/11/12/navy-seal-who-shot-usama-bin-laden-revealed-in-exclusive-fox-news-interview.html

Page 38, line 7: Finoa Roberts. "'For God and country – Geronimo, Geronimo, Geronimo': The words the SEAL who killed Osama Bin Laden radioed home – and why no-one will ever know his identity." Daily Mail. Published 2 August 2011. Retrieved 25 April 2016. http://www.dailymail.co.uk/news/article-2021260/Osama-Bin-Laden-Full-details-raid-catch-Al-Qaeda-leader-know-SEALs-identity.html

Page 41: Fox News. "Man who shot Usama bin Laden speaks out in exclusive Fox News interview." Published 12 November 2014. Retrieved 25 April 2016. http://www.foxnews.com/us/2014/11/12/navy-seal-who-shot-usama-bin-laden-revealed-in-exclusive-fox-news-interview.html. Page 48

Page 43, line 3: Fox News. "Man who shot Usama bin Laden speaks out in exclusive Fox News interview." Published 12 November 2014. Retrieved 25 April 2016. http://www.foxnews.com/us/2014/11/12/navy-seal-who-shot-usama-bin-laden-revealed-in-exclusive-fox-news-interview.html. Page 48

INDEX